# Memoirs Of The Life Of Scriblerus

## Jonathan Swift, Alexander Pope

# MEMOIRS

## OF THE

## L I F E

### OF

## *SCRIBLERUS.*

*Scalpellum, Calami, Atramentum, Charta, Libelli.*

By *D. S*————*t*.

*L O N D O N:*

Printed from the Original Copy from
*Dublin*; and Sold by *A. Moore* near
St. *Paul's.* MDCCXXIII.

# MEMOIRS, &c.

## OF

## SCRIBLERUS.

 A S I have a tender Regard to Men of great Merit, and fmall Fortunes, I fhall let flip no Opportunity of bringing them to Light, when either through a peculiar Mode-fty, or fome Unhappinefs in their Per-

B                    fonal

fonal Appearance, they have been un-
willing to prefent themfelves to the
World, and have been confequently no
otherwife remarkable in it, than by the
Number or Size of their Performances.
This Piece of Humanity was inftilled
into me by an accidental Turn in my
own Fortunes, which was owing to
the Difcovery a Man of great Pene-
tration and Power made of the Ex-
cellence and Superiority of my Genius;
and reflecting how much it was ob-
fcur'd by a Thread-bare Coat, very gra-
cioufly advanc'd me to a Station of
good Profit and little Trouble, any farther than to provide others to do my
Bufinefs. This gave me an Opportunity of cultivating my Perfon, which had
lain long unregarded, in which Branch
of my Profeffion I am fo confiderably
advanced, that I often over-hear the
Good Women, as I pafs by, cry out,
*L—d! how fleek our D—r is.* This
Piece

Piece of Flattery, with some other pri-
vate Reasons, not very material to in-
sert here, makes me advance twice a
Year to shew my Person and Parts,
for the Sake and Improvement of my
Male and Female Auditors; this ge-
nerally occasions Matter of mutual Compliment, and is the Support of a ci-
vil Correspondence the Year round.

Here you see an Instance of the Grand
Foible in human Nature, for which I
will not make any Apology, though I
have the greatest Authority of my Side;
my Design being at present to celebrate
a Person, whose Merit will employ all
the Stock of Genius I have collected,
so that begging the gentle Reader to
excuse these few Hints which I design
one Day to extend into a sizeable Vo-
lume, I shall, without farther Cere-
mony, conduct him out of the Entry
to the Place of Entertainment.

I

I say, proceeding upon this Principle,

*Haud ignara mali miseris succurrere disco.*

I have, in Justice to this worthy Gentleman, who (notwithstanding his Writings have furnish'd this our noble City with its politest Conversation for ten Years past) might otherwise have remain'd in Obscurity, collected some remarkable Circumstances of his Life, which I assure the Reader are related with all imaginable Truth and Accuracy.

The first of this antient Family that distinguish'd himself in the World was *Joachim Scriblerus*, a very learned Divine; he flourished in the Thirteenth and Fourteenth Centuries, and wrote an immense Quantity of very valuable Books in Divinity, of which there remain Thirty Two compleat Bodies, Seventy Six Commentaries, besides Two Thousand
sand

sand Differtations and feparate Treati-
fes; of which, a great Part were to
be feen in a curious Collection of moft
rare Books, fet forth in a neighbouring
Metropolis, by that Ingenious Gentleman, *Tom Rawlinfon*.

This *Joachim* had Seven Sons, who
were all educated under the Father till
they came of Age, but were then turn-
ed out to the wide World with a fuf-
ficient Quantity of Quills, and other
Implements, to get a Livelihood. But
as the Father was to portion out his
Stock into fo many equal Parts, nei-
ther of thefe young Gentlemen were
able to make any great Figure among
the *Literati*; fo that not one of the
Family broke out in any remarkable
Manner till the laft Century, when the
fcattered Genius * of the Family was
collected

* *Here it may not be improper to remark*
*the*

collected into the Hands of the only
Male Heir, to whose Life and Histo-
ry the curious Reader is desired to
attend.

*Timothy Scriblerus* was the Son of
an eminent Stationer, who for several
Years after Marriage was in Expectation of a Male Heir; Daughters he
had in Abundance, but his chief Concern was, least the Fame of the Family should dwindle for Want of a
Son, and the World should not know
he was any Relative of Old *Joachim.*
This made him frequently very pensive,
and

---

*the near Relation of Quills and Genius.
When a Man makes any bold Stroke in Rhime,
don't we cry, — That's a fine Flight, — he
soars; — that's a lofty Expression; — or, —
his Fancy is upon the Wing; finding the Sen-
tence always dignify'd by an Allusion to a
Goose-Wing, which shews the Preeminence, tho'
I compliment my Friend by making them sig-
nify the same.*

and one Day when he was more than ordinary fo, an elderly Woman obferving the Concern in his Countenance, came up to the Shop Door, and fhaking her Head, accofted him in the following Manner: I am very forry for your Misfortune, my good Mafter, but if you will crofs my Hand with a fmall Spill, and follow my Advice, you fhall have a Son to your Wifh before the Year is out. The Mention of a Circumftance that he could not imagine how fhe came acquainted with, encouraged him to gratify her in any Requeft, whereupon he defired her to fit down and proceed. You are to know then, Sir, faid fhe, that from my Acquaintance with the Stars I came by the Knowledge of your Wants; and by my great Skill in Natural Magick, to underftand the Method of fupplying them; provided you do your Part and follow this Direction: He promis'd ftrict Obfervance,

and

and received the following Prefcript :
Take Seven of the faireft Sheets of
Paper, and upon each of them you
muft have Seven Alphabets of Seven
different Languages varied Seventy Seven times, fo that no one Letter ftand
twice in the fame Pofture; when you
have done this, clip all thefe Letters
afunder, and few them up in a Pillowbier,
and upon a certain critical Conjuncture —

— — — — — — — — — — —

During this Operation the Pillow muft
be placed fo, that fhe may incline her-
felf towards the Right Side; I fuppofe
from that Hint of the Poet's,

*Virgam Dextra tenet* ———

The Good Man communicated this to
his Wife, and they took the firft Opportunity of following her Advice: Accordingly in Nine Months Time they
were in daily Expectation of Succefs.

It

It happen'd one Evening they were amu-
fing themfelves with the Profpect of
their Blifs, and laying Schemes for the
Education and Advancement of their
promis'd Heir ; the Converfation made
fuch an Impreffion upon the Woman
that fhe dreamt that Night the following Dream : She thought the Pains of
Child-bearing were coming upon her,
and order'd the Midwife to be fent
for, who no fooner enter'd the Room
but ran to her Affiftance, and immediately, with one dreadful Pang, out came
a monftrous Thing, which the Midwife taking to the Light, in a great
Fright, cry'd out, *L——d! what is
this?* And laying it down upon the
Table there iffued from it a great
Stream of Liquid, that divided itfelf
into ten thoufand little Branches, that
fpread themfelves over the whole Room:
This alarm'd the Company, which by
this Time fhe thought was grown very

numerous

numerous from the Flock of good Women that came to affift at her Labour; every body crowded to fee the young Progeny, when, to their horrid Amafement, they found it was a great black Inkhorn fending out innumerable Streams of Ink; this fo alarm'd her that fhe awaked.

In dreadful Confternation fhe continued the remaining Part of the Night, to think what could be the Event of fo uncouth a Dream; but in the Morning advifing with her Hufband, they determined to go to a Man in the next Street, who had great Skill in Dreams, and other Mifteries of Nature; accordingly up they got, and were heying to the Expounder, when they were met at the Door, by the fame good Woman, whofe advife they had followed with fuch Succefs; and immediately taking her by the Arm drew her in, and

desired

defired her Opinion of the Dream that had created in them fo many Fears, which they related as above, not omitting the leaft Circumftance. Here the Sallow Sorcerefs paus'd a while, then with a chearful Countenance, that difperfed half their Fears, began: The Inkhorn with thofe innumerable Streams iffuing from it, are the Types, or Symbols of his Genius, and the Extent of it; by them are fignify'd the great Variety of Productions in human Learning, that will render him the Admiration and Surprize of all the Univerfe; as to that Spout, it betokens the Sex, and that it will be a Son. Overjoy'd at this Interpretation they difmis'd her with a Reward, determining to wait the Event with Patience. In a few Days the Woman was brought to Bed of a Son, which affur'd them of the remaining Part; and now all their Hearts were fet upon, was the proper Method

C 2                    of

of educating it, leaft by any falfe Step
they fhould mar the great Genius that
was to be the Light of future Ages.
Long Time they confulted together,
at laft determin'd to watch the little
Motions of his Infancy, and learn from
them how beft to humour his Genius.
They obferv'd no Diverfion took fo
much with him as the ratling of Paper, and dabling in Ink, and that
young *Tim* was never better pleafed
than when up to the Elbows in it;
this they look'd upon as an Earneft of
what was promifed in the Dream, and
refolv'd to encourage him as far as their
Stock would permit. One Day the
Nurfe, with great Joy, came running
to the Father to tell him Mafter *Tim*
call'd Papa, but the Father foon found
the Miftake, and that the firft Word
*Tim* utter'd was, Paper. As *Tim*
advanc'd in Years, the manifeft bent
of his Genius determin'd the Father to

put

put him Apprentice to a Scrivener,
where he might learn to write a le-
gible and swift Hand, that his Invention might not wait for his Pen; which
was well judged, for I myself must
acknowledge that in the Heat of my
Imagination, I have had such a quick
Succeffion of beautiful Thoughts, that
for Want of Speed to reduce them to
Pen, Ink, and Paper, the World has
loft, I figh to repeat it, a moft valuable Treafure, both of Inftruction and
Entertainment. This was prudently a-
voided, for, by inceffant Practice, *Tim*,
in a little Time, wrote as faft as he
could think. The Father propos'd to
him Accounts, but *Tim* prudently told
him, he was refolv'd not to deal with
this World any more than from Hand
to Mouth, and begg'd that might not
interrupt his Progrefs in Affairs of grea-
ter Moment. Thus *Tim* fally'd out,
and in the two firft Years of his Ap-
prenticefhip

prenticeſhip he apply'd himſelf ſo dili-
gently to his Improvement, that, without interrupting his Maſter's Buſineſs, he
had tranſcrib'd 70 Volumes in Folio, of
different Languages; he could repeat by
Heart all the *Seven Wiſe Maſters* had
ſaid, he knew all the *Seven Cham-
pions Conquer'd*, and *the Hiſtory of
the Seven Wonders of the World*. He
had dipp'd into 7 Sciences, and began
now to be in Vogue among the People
of Letters. The diſtreſs'd of all Kinds
came to him to have their Caſes drawn
up, preferring *Tim* before his Maſter.
He had ſuch an eaſy Knack in the
Epiſtolary Way, that he could dreſs
up the Complaint of a forſaken Cham-
ber Maid in the moſt affecting Terms,
deſcribe the Caſe of a poor Invalid,
whether directed to a General, or a
Surgeon; in ſhort, all Caſes came before him, and he grew intimate with
the Town Intrigues, and learn'd be-
hind

hind the Defk, in a low Way, what he afterwards treated of in the fublime. *Tim* now began to think that Servitude was an Enemy to Great Minds, that they fhould not be cramp'd by low Indentures, left his Mafter, and returned to his Father, who gave him Entertainment in his Houfe, and, to keep his Genius in Play, allow'd him a Rheam of Paper, and a Quartern of Ink every Day: Tho' this was an expenfive Article, he was refolv'd to improve his Son's Talents at the Hazzard of his own Fortunes. So unbounded was the Genius of our young Student that he would one Day write a Syftem of Phyfick; the next, a Comedy, or Copy of Verfes; a third, would make a Sermon; the next, a Tale of a Tub, or Romance; but had this peculiar Turn in his Temper (whether it proceeded from natural Modefty, or Policy, I will not venture to determine)

that

that he never would own his Productions, but always father'd them upon
fome body or other: I remember a
Copy of his that appear'd under the
Name of *P——e*, wherein he com-
pliments a mufical Lady, but the World
found him out here, and tho' they look'd
upon it as one of his Juvenile Performances, every body faid it was pretti-
ly done for one of his Bignefs. *Tim*
now apply'd himfelf to his Studies fo
ftrictly that his Father was forced to
encreafe his Allowance: This fell fo
heavy upon him, and the Stock wafted
fo faft, that in a fhort Time he had
no Paper to ferve his Cuftomers; his
Trade fell off, he run to Decay, and
was forc'd to turn himfelf and his
Wife upon their Son for a Support from
that Genius they had fo carefully in-
dulg'd. *Tim* foon got him an Appart-
ment, any thing contented him fo he
had no Noife over his Head; but the

Altera-

Alteration in the Method of Life had such Effect upon the good old Couple, that they were both feiz'd with an Atrophy, and languifhing a few Days, dyed. Now the young Man being more at large than before, began to keep a little Company, and it was foon buzz'd about that *Tim* was the greateft Genius of the Age, and the Bookfellers began to hunt after him; fome offer'd Money, but he was fo great a Contemner of Mammon that he was never known to keep Company with more than a Tefter at once: They attack'd him different Ways to no Purpofe, *Tim* was refolv'd to ftand upon his own Bottom, knowing his Capacity would allow him to imitate the fublimeft Wits of his Time, and that a Title Page well countenanced would not fail of felling Three Editions at leaft. It happen'd unluckily about this Time that *Tim* fell fick of a Fever that fet-

tled

tled in his Head, and he would run up and down in Alleys and Corners affronting every Body : In this Mood a Friend of mine met him one Day, and *Tim* accosted him with an great Oath, Z——ds, Sir, Don't you know me? Not I indeed, Sir, quoth my Friend, very civilly. No, Sir, I am *J——n D——s* Sir, the only Man alive that has a true Taste of the Sublime. Sir, your most humble Servant, says my Friend, then you are not the Man I took you for. To convince you that I am, quoth *Tim,* stooping down to the Kennel, take that, and throws a great Handful of Mud all over his Cloaths. My Friend acknowledg'd his Mistake, and got out of his Reach as fast as he could. Another Time he collected a great Mob about him, and was telling them that those Letters the World call'd Mr. *Bull's* were not Mr. *Bull's,* and that he could prove they were wrote

Two

Two Thoufand Years before Mr. *Bull*
was ever thought of. Three or Four
Gentlemen paffing by over-heard *Tim*
talk in this extravagant Manner, and
defired him to keep his Temper a Mi-
nute and they wou'd convince him Mr.
*Bull* was the Man that wrote thofe
Letters. How! fays *Tim*, do you pre-
tend to contradict a Mafter of a Col-
lege, (for in thofe Vagaries he kept
to his Humour of perfonating fome Great
Man) I tell you, you are a Parcel of
ignorant blockheadly Dunces: Here he
fell a kicking, and flouncing, and fplafh-
ing, that the Company was glad to
make the beft of their Way, for
fear of worfe Ufage. In thefe Refve-
ries he continued a good while, till
Somebody put him into a Courfe of
Phyfick, and recovered him perfectly.
Now he fet himfelf to Work once more,
very gravely, for the Improvement of
Mankind; and fell upon Two Things.

The

The firſt was, to wipe out a Flaw in
Hiſtory that the World had paſſed by
for near 1700 Years; and, as a Matter of great Importance, he ſtudied
Night and Day to find Proofs to countenance this new and uſeful Invention.
Having ſettled the Thing to his Mind,
he took an Opportunity to tell the World
of what Importance it was to be ſet
right in the Affair under his Conſide-
ration; and after opening the Miſtake
to them, began to Reaſon with them
after this Manner: Look ye, Gentlemen, at the Time he lived, the Places
he dwell'd in were under the *Roman*
Jyriſdiction, and were governed by Lord
Lieutenants, ſo that he could have no
Kingdom under them; and if he had
a Mind to one by himſelf, he muſt
have travelled a great Way, Three
Parts of the known World being then
in their Dominions: But why ſtand I
to prove this? Gentlemen, here is my

Hand

Hand upon it, I have confidered the Thing ferioufly, and I proteft to you folemnly, *in verbo Sacerdotis*, as I hope to change this troublefome ———— Life for a better, he was fo far from having a Kingdom, that he had not one Foot of Land in all the World; and if either of us had been alive then, and in the fame Street, he would have had no more to do with us than the Emperor of *Ruffia* has at this Moment. Here *Tim* made his Bow, and left them to confider of it. Now, thinks he, I have made Way for a fine Argument; and obferving he had fet the People all agog, he thought this the critical Time to try the Extent of his Genius by managing this whole Argument himfelf, *Pro* and *Con*. Immediately he publifh'd an Anfwer to his former Affertion, proving that he was a King, and had great Authority upon Earth; and if he attempted to affert

fert the Contrary, he would put him in the C———s, and convince him to his Coft. And now the Storm began to thicken; one Day he would publifh, *A Vindication of, &c.* Another, *A Letter to, &c.* A Third, *A Defence of, &c.* Sometimes calling himfelf * ———, or ———, or ———, or ———, or ———, giving a new Name to every Treatife, and the whole Town began to be in an Uproar for Fear of Daggers drawing, for he would give the Lye again and again, and appeal to three or four at a Time, of each Side, to prove each lied. And tho' he frequently ufed Language below a Porter, yet he reafon'd fo much like a Divine, produc'd fo many ftrong Arguments, and couch'd fo much Artifice

---

* *Here was a Lift of Rt. Rds. Rds. and M. As. which the Bookfeller thinks fit to leave out.*

tifice on each Side the Queftion, that not one of them all refufed to own his Productions; but every body fwore their Adverfaries were ————. The Town continu'd in the Miftake, and leaft they fhould any longer, and in Honour to my Friend, I take this Opportunity of affuring them they were every one wrote with his own Hand.

The Second was, he having run through all Uviuerfal Syftems of Phylofophy, and traced Nature in all her Intricacies, was fo familiar with every Operation fhe was Miftrefs of, knew the Neceffity of her acting in the regular Manner fhe does, that he had convinc'd himfelf there was no Occafion for a fuperior Power; and that this Piece of ufeful Knowledge fhould not be kept a Secret from the World, he oblig'd them with his Reafons in feveral very elaborate Difcourfes, under

the

the Names of *T—d*, *C——s*, *C—o*;
to which the *Beau Monde* are vaſtly
beholden for the moſt agreeable Set of
Morals they ever put in Practice.

I have not been able to collect all
the ſcatter'd Pieces of his, for Want
of Time and proper Correſpondents,
tho' I muſt not omit three curious little
Tracts of P—ns, F——ts, and D—d—
—ns, all ſurprizing Pieces of Wit and
Ingenuity; with theſe he complimented
Dr. *S——ft*, which, tho' they were too
gay for one of his Cloth, might have
ſet him up for a Wit, had not the
World known that his Talent lay more
in ſound Divinity that Rapartee.

I ſhall take my Leave of the Reader, intreating him, Firſt, not to con-
ſider theſe Memorandums as a perfect
Hiſtory; that was not what I promi-
ſed, but only look upon it as the To-
ken

ken of a Heart full of Gratitude towards a Man I acknowledge myself,
to the laft Degree, beholden to. That
I could not write for Fame he will
be affur'd, when he reflects upon the
Incapacity I have all along difcover'd
to do Juftice to my Friend, and I
hope no body will defcend to fufpect
me of any Thing elfe.

I muft obviate one Reflection I am
aware of, *viz*. *That there is not one
Word in the whole Book in different
Character*, by faying, that in true
Hiftory there is no Room for Humour
or Wit; and I muft own I have fti-
fled feveral very pretty Turns, for no
other Reafon than that they were below the Dignity of the Subject.

*F I N I S.*

## *Just publiſh'd,*

THE Wonderful Wonder of Wonders: Or, The Hole-Hiſtory of the Life and Actions of Mr. *Breech,* the Eighth Wonder of the World. Being an accurate Deſcription of the Birth, Education, Manner of Living, Religion, Politicks, Learning, *&c.* of mine A—ſe. By Dr. *S———t.* With a Preface, and ſome few Notes, explaining the moſt difficult Paſſages.

*Then as a Jeſt for this Time let it paſs,*
*And he that likes it not, may kiſs my A——*
JO. HAYNES.

The Sixth Edition. Printed from the Original Copy from *Dublin,* and Sold by *A. Moore* near St. *Paul's.*

Ingram Content Group UK Ltd.
Milton Keynes UK
UKHW050802270323
419227UK00009B/594